BORN TO CHANGE

Tiffany Robinson

Copyright

ISBN-13: 978-0692456620 (Too Real LLC.)
ISBN-10: 0692456627

Born To Change
Headshot Photography by: Roderick Smith
Published by: Too Real LLC.
Marietta, GA 30008
Printed in the United States of America

Note: This book is intended to give you hope for your life and how to be at peace while making a change in your life. Readers are advised to reach out for further help if needed before making any changes with your life. The information in this book is based on the author's belief and experiences in life. The author cannot be held responsible for any actions that may be encountered.

Dedication

This book is dedicated to you from my heart to your heart. To help you feel encouraged about your future life while gaining a relationship with GOD and LOVING yourself at the same time. I also want you to know that whatever the DEVIL has stolen from you, GOD is going to replace it.

"Life is full of greatness when you are full of life."

-Tiffany Robinson

Acknowledgements

I would first like to thank GOD for giving me the strength to overcome all strongholds that were in my life, that were trying to keep me away from living the life GOD has created for me. Just to know that GOD has a better plan for my life gives me the hope to look forward to the future which also keeps my FAITH in believing in HIM. If it wasn't for GOD I would be nothing. I can't express enough how THANKFUL I am and the LOVE I have for HIM. I feel so blessed that he has filled me with so much LOVE for the world to be a vessel for HIM. I also would like to thank my mother for always being there for me no matter what and NEVER turning her back on me. She has taught me the true meaning of being a mother without explaining. Just her actions alone have been more of an understanding than words. Mom, I love you always and forever.

I can't forget about my father he is everything a daughter could ask for. He has taught me so many things in life that he doesn't even realize. I love you for that! Most importantly I want to give a BIG THANK YOU to my husband for supporting me on my journey— from seeing me grow from the world to Christ and believing in me with all his HEART. Oh, how he makes me feel so special! I love you!!! No words can ever amount to the love I have for my daughters. I am so thankful to have two beautiful healthy girls in my life. I do want to give a special shout out to my oldest daughter Endya for being such a great big sister and being very respectful to herself and others. You are the best pre-teen a mother could ask for. I love you my first born. My baby girl E'mani gets a special shout out for being a great helper wherever she goes. She has so much love inside of her and she already knows how to spread it! I love you baby girl. I know that without having my own big sister, I wouldn't know what to do —she use to let me get on her nerves to the max and let me go everywhere with her and her friends and without a doubt I know she didn't want me to go LOL...Thanks Big Sis I love you. I really don't know where to begin with my big brother but I do know where it ends and that is, he was the one in my life to give me the best advice on boys growing up and he made sure I respected myself in life, just because of you that's why I am married to my middle school, high school sweetheart! Love you always and forever. Franklin White you know I am not going to forget about you, you are the best hands down thanks for your help to make my book be everything I wanted!!! There are also so many more people that have been a part of my journey, you know who you are and I love each and every one of you.

Contents

Born To Change

GOD knows better than anybody that for me to take time out of my daily life– from my beautiful family and motherly duties, then to somehow place my thoughts in a written format to hopefully inspire and motivate others is very important to me. From the outset, I was sure that to complete this project it was going to take everything I had. That's why every step of the way of this process, I have made sure GOD has been not only a part of this journey but the driving force behind it.

As long as I can remember I have always been the one person, amongst my family, friends and collogues who they have continually come to in their time of need to get advice or help in difficult situations. I never thought in a million years that just by helping others with sharing my wisdom and insight on their pressing matters would help them to gain clarity in their life situations. After receiving plenty of prodding from those I would give my advice to, I began to listen to their view of what they all saw in me and I finally realized it was a gift from GOD and a blessing for me that I couldn't ignore.

We all want to discover our GOD given talent in our lives. The talent of being patient, a good listener and being able to give an honest opinion without judging is what HE has bestowed on me and it has truly been a BLESSING. As I have accepted my gift I have completely grew with all the challenges that have came my way with the strength that GOD has blessed all us with. To this point my purpose has become the provision of my life as a Life Coach, Motivational Speaker and most importantly a Woman of GOD.

My main goal in writing this book is to assist anyone who wants to implement change in their lives and remove themselves from being the same wrong lane person– day after day. I'm talking about those who have realized that what they thought was working in their life at one time or another actually was not working and realized their reality wasn't real and no longer working for them. Those who have come to that conclusion have already reached the first step into a better life and my intentions for writing this book is to provide wisdom and guidance so that the same mistakes and choices that are being made in our lives on a constant basis are not made over and over again and we together, will break the cycle and move on towards our destined life.

However I do understand that it is very difficult to change. I have learned that when a person is living their life in a certain way other than what we know deep down inside it isn't pleasing to ourselves as well as those around us and most certainly not to GOD. It is apparent that we all need to change in our lives as our spirit tries to guide us in the right direction but we as humans don't always know how to follow.

Also part of my goal with this book is to help my readers obtain the positive change, just like the trainer who transforms people who has never taken care of their bodies or for example like a doctor who is recommending nicotine patches to help a patient quit smoking cigarettes. Not only did I set goals for my readers but most importantly to obtain what they are searching for to live a more peaceful, loving and prayerful life.

I have been through much in my life and I have not always been that person to follow in the right direction but now I'm praising while thanking GOD that I have become the person that HE has created me to be. There is nothing better than living and giving PEACE and LOVE. When those two things are in my life there is absolutely nothing else that matters. That's not to say that I have always given peace and love and didn't have to make changes in my life because I have.

At one point in my life my attitude was so bad that I could hardly stand to be around myself. For years, I walked around confused as to why this change had to happen in my life in my teen years which also affected my early adulthood. I carried the most unimaginable turmoil that anyone could feel. But due to GOD's Grace I realized that Satan is not going to give us anything good to do and that is why it is so important to be in tune with your spirit and recognize how to close down anything that is not welcoming to yourself and GOD instead of continually acting or doing the same thing over and over again and that's why I believe, **We Were Born To Change.**

I want those reading my book to realize that life is so much more than what we make it. Life is given to be enjoyed and lived with a purpose but many of us live our lives the way someone else has prescribed for us to live. Sometimes we try to reach that place that someone else has ordained and designed for us and we make life a terrible place and in the process we push ourselves away from GOD and life becomes much worse than it was intended to be.

Today in these times, life moves with blinding speed. I am realizing that things are quickly getting out of control leaving many people who are searching for a purpose in life, very confused and angry because of the fact they do not realize that change in their life is the only way they will begin to enjoy their lives and do the things they actually want to do in life.

As a little girl I never went to church but I always wanted to know more about GOD. I remember times when I couldn't wait until Sunday so I could watch church on television or just play church all by myself and talk to GOD. For a reason that I cannot explain, I have always been close to GOD. I don't remember who told me about GOD growing up as a child, but I know that I have always felt HIS presence and have been able to talk to him in my darkest hour. In those ways as a child I always knew I was different. I don't blame my parents for not taking me to church but I am very grateful for HIS spirit and allowing it to take over my mind, body, soul and the way I choose to live my life.

If you only learn one thing after reading this book, I hope that you realize that the more things you go through just as I have been through—GOD will guide you to the right place just as HE has done for me.

You Can't Run From It Face It

I have grown to realize that what has happened in my life has shaped the person I have become and person I will turn out to be. I will always remember the time when my parents told me that they were getting a divorce. Of course at the time I was a teen but I was totally blindsided about their decision and never saw it coming because in *my* mind everything between my parents was fine and our life as a family unit couldn't be better.

Even as a little girl I can remember that I always valued family so very much so that the revelation of my parent's divorce was quite hard for me to accept and understand. As a teenager when I found out about their separation all I wanted to *do* was *not do,* the right thing. After some time after this drastic change in my life, I realized that I was at a point where I was stuck. There wasn't anything that I could do about the situation but go with the flow of the things happening in my life. No, I didn't like the sudden change in my families' circumstances but I was just too young at the age of thirteen to do anything about it. I had no choice in any matters involving my family but that's when I can recall that the experience was still a turning point in my life. I learned to begin to live ahead of myself and not in the past; meaning I would put the thoughts of what I wanted out of my life in full view so that I could obtain them, no matter what I was going through.

So many of us when a storm comes we are so quick to blame everyone connected to the situation instead of dealing with the problem with a level headed mindset that will actually help you get through the situation. If we continue to look back at the past instead of looking towards the future there is no possible way to become free from the pain and confusion you are going through. Instead of creating more drama when a storm comes into existence that is when it is time for you to face reality and face what you are up against head-on.

I am not saying that dealing with problems that occur are easy but there is a point when we have to realize that the person who is in charge of the ultimate decision process in a crisis is the one who is actually going through the storm and dealing with the consequences of the situation.

Asking "why" and running around with the mindset of trying to figure out "why" something is happening to you is a wasted emotion that you can do without. Asking "why" does nothing but bring more confusion into the situation because first of all, you're trying to figure out a puzzle that you don't have all the pieces to; instead of dealing with the puzzle, place the pieces together. Also the time spent on something you don't have the answer to will only prolong the anguish of the situation and torture you mentally.

Getting to a point where you can stand up and face your problem only will come with believing that GOD will take over and lead you in the right direction. Surrendering to HIM will allow you to get it right. Admit that you need HIS help and step out of the way and resign to HIS will.

I know that a lot of people like to go to their friends when they have issues and problems but having friends are a good thing if you have level headed friends who you know deep down in your heart will comfort and help you go in the right direction. But a lot of times we have friends who relish in the fact that something or someone in your life has done you wrong. They like to pretend as if they're helping you get on the right path but are telling you the wrong turn to make, which only makes your problems more confusing in your mind. GOD won't do that because he already knows what you are going through.

I became pregnant at a very young age and at every turn and new situation that I encountered, I was being told to do things that were not in line with my spirit, heart and GOD. During the process of being pregnant it wasn't like I wasn't listening to the people who were much older than I was when they gave me their opinion on how I should handle my pregnancy. But when you are faced with a situation and you can feel that your spirit and heart are becoming affected by your decision there is only one place to turn and that is to GOD because in due time HE will open new doors for your life.

Realizing You're in the Wrong Lane

Everyone is unique and has individual gifts that serve a purpose that were giving to us by GOD. Some people are able to realize their GOD given gifts and are able to share them with the world but unfortunately there are some who live everyday of their lives traveling down the wrong lane and never are able to get things the way GOD destined them to be.

A lot of the time the devil is able to trick us by placing our focus on what others have and what they are doing by making it seem as though the road they are traveling is for us even when it's full of sin and deceit. He tricks us by attempting to get us to travel the same path regardless of what our heart tells us and if we choose to follow the path, the pathway only leads to confusion and turmoil on our way to our desired destination.

Being able to realize and accept the way GOD wants you to live your life is what will make you truly feel alive and place you on your own individual right path for your life. Comparing yourself or placing yourself into competition with others and attempting to walk in their path to achieve is not living your life, it's being an imposter of someone else's life.

Embracing our own life and journey is so important. Understanding that when we focus on others we are placing too much attention on their lives than our own and what we should be accomplishing. Stepping outside our own path only places us in a repetitive revolving cycle that never stops. You will know when you're on the right path because your heart will tell you so and you will be on a constant steady course that doesn't travel left nor right or round and round in a loop. When you realize you are on the right path you will not question yourself about the direction you're headed or what you're doing in the process because you have let GOD take control.

It is important to let your heart be the determining factor of realizing that you are on the right path. No longer will the feelings of jealousy or being in competition with others affect you. When you are on the right path it will not matter to you what someone else is doing. When we travel in our own lane there is no desire to be in anyone else's business or life because you are busy following your own heart and being about your own business.

I have never proclaimed that getting in "Your" lane would be a swerve in the road but it will take focus to get in the right lane. If it was easy then there would be less drama and turmoil in the world and the devil would be out of business, but that is not the case. The first thing that must be done to get on the right path on your journey is that you must confess. Confess and admit to yourself so you can realize that what you're doing or haven't been doing isn't the right way. It is very important that you confess in a way that is uplifting to your spirit so that you aren't making yourself feel bad about the road you were on because confessions are meant to move us in the right direction.

Secondly you have to take all the negativity away from your daily life. I can't count how many clients I have coached who have had to make the decision to move away from friends, associates and even some family members who were constantly negative in their life just as I have done myself, in order to get in the right lane. In addition you have to remember and understand that this journey of putting yourself on the right path is between you and GOD. In your heart you have to realize right away if something is not for GOD then it is not for you. You are your very own brand and pressure from outside forces that attempt to throw you off your path must be dealt with as quickly as they come into your life because the enemy will not waste any time trying to keep you in the wrong lane at every chance.

Lastly, you have to make your word your bond in order to set yourself up to move in another lane. It will take more than just confessing and stripping the negativity out of your life. Keeping your word to make the change to move into the right lane is the most important and difficult of all. It will be challenging because after making up your mind to do a new and better thing in your life, thoughts of how things "use" to be always find their way of reoccurring in your life.

The only way to make things happen in life is action on our part. We have to remember that there is a beginning and an end to what we want to accomplish. Moving in a positive direction in life has to be done on a day to day basis and there is no other way around it. We must work to better ourselves from sun up to sun down, one day at a time to achieve our goals. The more we achieve our goals to getting on the right path, living in righteousness will become easier and easier.

Hearing GOD's Voice

There is no other way to put this, GOD is my source of direction on my journey. In my life I have learned to put all my trust in GOD and not to depend on man. It's so important to put GOD first and foremost in your life so you will understand when he speaks to you. Truthfully he speaks to us all the time and when we listen we are rewarded and when we don't we only will continue down a path of confusion.

Paying close attention to your inner voice and spirit as it communicates with you is very important. I am certain that GOD comes into our lives to give us instructions on what steps to take next but it is our choice to either follow them or not. So many people have testified about following GOD'S voice which have put them right where they needed to be, not to mention it was right on time for what was going on in their life at the moment.

The only way to hear from GOD is to talk with GOD. We do this by praying, praising and worshiping HIM every day. There is no other way around it, if GOD is going to speak to you, you must speak with him. A great way to start talking to HIM would be taking time out of our daily schedules to sit down and have a conversation with HIM, the same way as talking with your friends catching up on the latest "tea."

A lot of times we are busy with our daily lives that it seems to be to hectic to take the time out for GOD and we let it slip our minds. We have to realize that the time for HIM is just like what we make for anything else in our life. Not only is the time with HIM important but it also needs to take place where you can really free yourself because HIS words breathe life into our souls.

We do make mistakes a lot of the time when we don't choose to listen to God. It's not that we don't want to listen we are just accustomed to holding onto what's familiar so that we can stay in our comfort zone, when actually it's not the "comfort zone" that we are covered by it's the GRACE OF GOD. Your inner voice will always confirm that what you have going on isn't for you, however we do ignore the truth because we aren't ready to do the right thing which keeps us caught up in the foolishness that GOD is trying to address.

One more time, one more time is one of the devils favorite suggestion when he knows you are listening to GOD and attempting to do the right thing in your life. When the enemy sees that you are searching for true answers to make permanent changes in your life and once you start listening to your heart and spirit; without fail the enemy will attack you with all types of reasons why you should continue to do the wrong things instead of listening to the spirit of GOD leading you to the right thing.

This is one of the reasons I named this book **Born to Change** because I am living proof that GOD is real so I wanted to share my testimony because I see where in so many areas the devil has the world turned backwards to keep us away from GOD's voice that's in our hearts which is the place where we can make the change by not just listening to our inner voice but following HIS direction when we hear HIM.

I talk a lot about different phases that we experience in life that causes us to question where we are headed on our journey. When I first set out to write this book I had to set fear aside and listen to GOD's voice that was directing me to step out on faith to push me to go to another level. I knew I was going to have to accomplish what GOD put on my heart. When I finally decided to listen and put my plan in motion, the devil attempted to attack me with thoughts like, "*Your testimony is not good enough and why would you want to spend your time telling people about the goodness of GOD*"? But his tricks didn't work nor did I fall weak to allow him to destroy my vision that GOD had for me and I never will.

It is so important to understand that when your spirit is telling you what to do— don't run from it, instead embrace it and follow its lead. If you believe in your heart that your vision and your spirit are leading your life in a certain direction then follow it. Just ask yourself the question, *"What am I living for, if I don't have anything to live for?"* The unseen you will see it and the unknown will be known, needless to say that's what you call having FAITH.

It's Not What You Know

It's who you know

(GOD)

It is a known fact that people don't like going to church anymore. Regretfully the church has become a place where people go to get a motivational speech to keep them motivated for what's taken place in their life at the moment along with giving them hope for their dreams to come true for the future. With that being said, church is so much more than that, we should leave church feeling the true word of GOD in our soul to give us a closer relationship with him. That's why it's so important to know GOD before going to church more than expecting the pastor to be GOD because in reality we are all human trying to gain the true meaning of living here on earth.

Your life will become so much more peaceful when you actually know GOD instead of hearing about GOD and what he can do in your life. When you know GOD you will feel the relationship with him. It's like a natural high when you realize that he is with you forever and not temporary. Once you allow him into your life you will notice that your life is less stressful and uplifting not just in your life, but also those around you.

For some reason it's hard for people to understand GOD because they don't really take the time out as if they would with someone that they would want to see themselves being with. Their way of life has been without him for so long that they become afraid of the change that is required to fully understand him. GOD actually wants you to give your life to him not take it from him.

Without a doubt it is difficult for people to believe to have FAITH in GOD'S word. It's just the type of world we live in that no one will believe anything until they see it and won't go beyond believing in their own vision. That is the main reason why people are supporting so many other brands of spirituality and religion.

It's truly hard for me to understand why it's so hard for people to see that GOD actually wants you to give your life to him. He wants to be your best friend that you can come to for any reason and be the SOURCE for all of your needs. I have realized it's because some people try to quench their spiritual thirst by physical and material means such as their family, friends, relationships, jobs and the things they have. It never fails that I will come across those who have a great job, nice house, family and everything else, but they constantly complain about those things. Complain about their boss, complain about their partner, complain about the new car they just purchased but I am a witness that when you know GOD and understand the goodness, the peace love and happiness HE can bring into your life all forms of complaining and feeling uneasy will cease.

Please understand that the devil finds a way to bless you too. He blesses you in ways to keep you in bondage and will keep you in a state of being where you never feel satisfied even though you might have attained some of the finer things in life. But there is one thing that the devil can't give you and that is PEACE.

I'm asked the question all the time, how to receive and achieve PEACE. What I do is think what's ahead for me instead of thinking about what's going on. I personally don't like being put under pressure about things that I know isn't in my hands but yet I have to make choices as if they were. What I mean about that, is I know that GOD has total control over all things but yet I still have to make all the actions to show that I know who's in control without explaining myself.

I believe that we are on this earth to share our testimonies and I have plenty to share but this is one that was an eye opener for me. As a child I went to church with a friend for Halloween. When we arrived at the church we had to pick a ticket and on the tickets it said either HEAVEN or hell. When I picked my ticket my ticket had Hell on it, so I had to go to a place they had set up as Hell. When I walked in there it was really hot. I noticed that they had all of the things we would call the "good life" inside. There was the latest rap music, hot wings and soda. After I spent some time inside, my friend was able to come get me out to go to HEAVEN only because I was a guest and her ticket had heaven on it. When I walked inside of HEAVEN the temperature was more comfortable, I could hear gospel music while we had fruit and juice. It was just so very peaceful and uplifting. Just like one of my goals with my life and this book.

Living In HIS Direction

It's a battle to live here on earth no matter if you are living in GOD'S direction or following the path of the enemy, but I do know that the battle is worth it living for him. A lot of times when people come to me they know that I will be #TOOREAL with them and let them know this may not be what you want to hear but "GOD has the answers to all your questions." Not only am I telling others that but I live by that. Those are the directions of faith that I have; just like the person who likes to listen to a GPS while knowing they know the direction all along, but yet still, follows the GPS anyway then ends up late for an appointment because of the closed roads the GPS didn't know about.

When I follow GOD's direction life is less worrisome because I don't have to second guess myself. The more you are following GOD's direction you become more in command of your choices because you are pleasing GOD. Some people allow themselves to get caught up in the religious aspect of knowing GOD but not serving GOD.

I maintain that there is only one GOD and Holy Spirit and religion is used as a vessel for people to get in touch with GOD. But there are times when religion steps out of boundaries with what GOD intends for us and it becomes dangerous to our souls because it veers off the path of GOD's grace and what he intended for our lives.

If you are still able to wake up then there is no doubt that GOD has a plan for your life. We must be certain that we don't waste our precious seconds, minutes, hours and days on earth. That's why it is important to understand that GOD is the only way. Not just religion because today religion on earth is one of man's major problems here. There are way too many people committing crimes in the name of their religion that promotes their GOD which leads to differences and disputes. I am of PEACE, LOVE, HAPPINESS of GOD and the HOLY SPIRIT.

Reality vs. Fake Reality

There is a very strong spirit in society that has a lot of mindsets trapped and confused in what is *real* and what is not *real* in our daily lives. From the time that we wake up in the morning, until the time we go to bed at night, our brains are blasted with information and images of a cast of fake realities and images that we have become accustomed to by our radio, television and internet outlets and at the same time can't decipher if it's real or not.

The spirit of this fake reality has gained strength throughout the years and on any given night millions of uncovered souls sit and watch on television the fairytale lives of people who are paid to portray a scripted lifestyle that is very negative and does more harm than good to the viewers.

GOD gives us the ability to know when we are not being shown something on a practical and truthful level. So we need to use our GOD given common sense and understanding of reality, when we watch reality shows. There are way too many people who have made these characters on these television shows their role models. Unfortunately, when they attempt to act out and portray the characters in the same manner then; REALITY strikes and they realize that they have made a mistake by following a destructive path that the devil has laid out for them.

Recently, more and more shows are appearing on television that are attacking GOD's kingdom as those who have been in a position to help lead us to him— have now caused a misleading path for GOD's children for fame and fortune. It becomes very difficult to tell someone that what they are doing is not in line with GOD when they see it happening in the lives of people who are supposedly leaders in GOD's kingdom here on earth. But I know sure as there is a GOD, that GOD will surely not take kindly to the foolishness and thirst for fame by those he has blessed to magnify HIS kingdom in HIS name lightly on judgment day.

Also the reality of being real when it comes to our looks and bodies and the great lengths we go through to enhance and uplift what we already have has gotten out of control. I do understand how important it is to keep yourself up and to maintain your body. But the key word is "yourself" not injections, lifts and tucks. We need to uplift our minds instead of our behinds with chemicals that we don't know the long term effects.

These are many of things we need to work on when it deals with being real and living a fake life.

It ultimately comes down to living a fairytale and that is surely not, what GOD wants us to do. He has blessed us with what he wants us to have and how he wants us to look. When we try to deviate from what HE has created for our lives we are out of order and living in confusion.

Everything that looks good isn't necessarily good for you. The time we are spending on obtaining attention by man is the same time we should be seeking to spend with GOD. If ever there is a time that we move away from living outside of our reality, it is now.

Changing our ways in these areas and asking GOD for direction and listening to HIM and reading his word is the only way. The only thing GOD wants us to do is uplift his HOLY NAME with praise. Absolutely nothing great can come from living a fairytale the rest of the days of our lives. I pray for the people who have been caught up in the "fake" reality that they will open their eyes and see what GOD really has for them. I also pray to GOD that he continues to give me the strength to humble myself to stay in line with the life that he has created for me.

I don't care if I stay behind the scenes all my life and never reach any level of fame. Being on television or becoming famous is not my goal. I just want to help people to get this message so their lives won't be so complicated. My mission is to inspire, inform and let people know about the goodness of GOD and all HE can do in your life.

No One Can Change You But You

I have always felt like we were meant to be Born to Change because if we somehow stay the same on our journey we would never see our true selves the way GOD created. Making a change in your thought process will help you see things in a different way so that you can clear your heart from bitterness to have a relationship with GOD. Even though coming to a point of deciding and realizing a change in life is necessary, it is no easy matter because most of the time we are dealing with habits and the only way a habit can end is to replace it with a new habit. We are the creators of any choices that we make in our life and when we decide to change we will start to realize that it is a battle within, especially when we try to do different and live a better life. Now as we move forward with our change our transformation will go from being stuck in the world to moving closer to Christ.

Knowing that we are the creators of our habits then it's obvious that we can be the ones who can stop partaking in the habit. Changing your attitude about any situation or habit that you know deep inside your spirit that isn't good for you which is currently playing a part in your life must come first. Realizing that your attitude is the most important element when it comes to change is paramount in order for your situation to become a positive reality where you can begin to do a new thing.

As I mentioned before, my attitude was not always the best. I am not proud of it but there was a time where I would curse someone out in a heartbeat if I felt it was needed. I eventually realized that my attitude was not getting me anywhere so with a lot of patience and hard work I became the type of person who avoids at all cost any type of confrontation and I feel it has been better for my spirit.

I do believe though that it is difficult to change habits after doing the same thing over and over again. When you do something every day it becomes your lifestyle and when you embed a habit in your everyday living it makes it that much harder to break away from the stronghold that has developed throughout your being.

After a stronghold has planted itself inside of your daily life it becomes a battle between you and the habit; but with the natural born strength that GOD has birthed inside of you, it will help you break the stronghold. Next must be your mindset about everything you want to change because once you place your mind on changing and you have a very strong attitude about change then you are at a point of winning and making the desired change you want to have in your life.

As I have already stated in an earlier chapter you must have a vision in order to see yourself already changed into what you want so that you can draw motivation from what you see. The vision is necessary and GOD will provide the provision for whatever you want to achieve.

My personal change in life that I had to make was very unique because I had to change at a very young age. I had to change due to me becoming a teen mom it was the most challenging thing I have ever had to do in my life. The change from a teen who could basically do whatever she wanted into a person who was now responsible for another living soul was not an easy adjustment. I had to change my entire way of living around. From the time that I woke up in the morning until the time I went to bed at night was now different. The change that I had to make was mandatory for me and my child. If I didn't follow GOD's wisdom and listen to HIM as HE always let me know that even though I was going through a difficult time, that I had a purpose in life and I am sure writing this book is part of HIS purpose for me to share with others.

When someone comes to hire me as their life coach; I know firsthand that the person is truly ready to make a change in his or her life. It takes the individual person to step outside the box and be committed to change to become a better person so that you can live a better life.

I am aware that some people need to take baby steps in order to grow and that is okay, we all grow on different levels but are trying to meet up at the same place. Progress through a process is what will ultimately help you not only change or break a stronghold in your life but show you how strong of a person you really are.

When The Enemy Attacks

In my opinion anything that goes against GOD's will is spiritual warfare. When you are facing generational curses and everyday battles of anything negative becomes spiritual warfare that we must keep at bay. Spiritual warfare comes by the way of the enemy. One of the great examples I like to use is, when you wake up in the morning and declare it will be the best day ever and as soon as you step foot out the door all hell breaks loose.

There are many different ways the enemy will attack, especially when you are attempting to change your life the way I have discussed in this book. Fear will be the first type of spiritual warfare that the enemy launches at you to get you back to doing the wrong thing. Fear will be there every step of the way no matter what you are trying to accomplish. Fear attacked me on so many levels when it came to writing this book. It attacked me and told me that I was not ready, no one wanted to read about what I had to say and that my testimony didn't matter to anyone. But I have declared and proven that the devil is a liar and what GOD has for me is for me without any disruptions by spiritual warfare.

Deception is another form of spiritual warfare that we must guard ourselves against. Deception is dangerous because it can lead us into a false direction that we shouldn't travel in and lead us into a phony sense of being and before we know it we are in a place of confusion and turmoil. I always like to use the example of a person who joins a church and is mislead by the leader not preaching the gospel and using the church for their own benefit instead of feeding souls. This is a very misleading path and something GOD did not intend for anyone to be a part of. That is why we need to make sure that we know GOD so that our spirit can identify the people in leadership positions because these are people who are typically persuasive and can easily manipulate minds.

Accusation is another form of spiritual warfare that we must guard our spirit from and understand how it occurs and creeps into our lives. In our lives we all have committed a sin, there are things in our past that we aren't too proud of or even may wish we could take them back. But sometimes when it comes to spiritual warfare in the realm of accusation, the enemy always tries to find ways to remind us constantly what we have done in our past and continue to remind us of it so that we can be bound by it and unable to move on with a clear conscience. The enemy's attack is one of guilt and shame. The enemy will place a guilty conscience in our minds where if we let it we will continue to carry our transgressions with us and pound it into our minds nonstop.

I saved the next and most critical form of spiritual warfare for last because this type of spiritual warfare is what opens the doors to all of our sins. Temptation is what the enemy uses to get inside of our lives. The enemy will prod, poke, push, jab and nudge us into doing the wrong thing anytime of the day or whenever the enemy sees an opening in our lives. The enemy tries to encourage us by placing things in our path that are no good for our lives and tries to trick us into thinking that these things are good for us even though we know they are not.

That is why it is so important to be connected to GOD so that HE can help us navigate through spiritual warfare traps that can destroy our lives. Spiritual warfare is not temporary it is definitely an everyday battle. Being aware of the strongholds and knowing how to quickly go to GOD to put them into submission is very important. When we are attacked we must place our defensive armor of GOD to protect us so that we can continue living an awesome life of love and peace without these types of interruptions to our spirits.

Feeling of No Support

There are many different instances and situations in life that we may feel like we don't have the proper support in our lives when it comes to assistance or some type of helping foundation from others to help us sustain problems that we may encounter. There are some people who like to just work problems and situations out on their own and there are others, who like to discuss problems and situations with friends and family to help them see their way for a clearer picture of what they are going through.

Lastly, there are those who do not feel they have any type of support and do not know where to turn.

I always will maintain that GOD is my main vessel for support. For me HE is my source no matter what I am going through. When I am going through a challenging situation I find a quiet place to sit and talk to HIM about how THANKFUL I am for all things and that I know he has the best solution for what he already knows I am going through. I do understand though, that you cannot walk through life without any interaction with friends and family. I am a living testament that there are times when GOD will direct you to your friends and family in your time of need for support may it be morale or material. I was blessed to have a couple of family members who helped me get through a very difficult time in my life.

Morale support by family and friends should always be taken as that. It is important to tread lightly to be able to realize that some support may not be what you want or need that's why it is important to make sure that the person offering support, genuinely has your best interest at heart. Also when stepping out and letting someone into your situation it is vital that the person is aware that you don't want them to actually solve a problem for you. It can be very frustrating when you go to someone to just "talk" and that person automatically knows how to solve "your" situation for you when in fact all you wanted to do was to discuss the situation for someone to listen so that maybe you can get a better sense of the problem yourself.

If you ever find yourself in need of support financially I think that it is a good idea, to go to the person you are seeking help from with a plan. When I was in need of a place to stay when I was pregnant with my second child after I lost my first apartment, I had to come up with a plan. I didn't want to be a burden to my aunt and her family who opened their basement to me, so I did what I had to do. I wasn't able to give them a lot of money, so I gave what I could while saving all that I needed in order to move out as soon as possible, at the same time. The plan was difficult and very challenging but I accomplished what I set out to do and I felt encouraged for whatever was coming my way thereafter. I would tell anyone to be very careful when offering support that will help someone get through challenging situations. I would advise someone in this situation to take the persons bad problem and turn it into the most positive situation possible. I would also use the blueprint that I have used in solving my own problems by helping them devise a plan to help work out their situation. Ask questions that will make them reach deep into their situations and really think about the best possible solutions that will make their lives better. You can also share a bit about your own personal experiences then ask them to think outside the box to handle their situations.

Prayer Changes Things

If I was asked what prayer was to me I would answer that it was genuine communication with GOD. My answer would be that it gives me STRENGTH, JOY AND HOPE while spending time LOVING, PRAISING with the most HIGH. I always love to talk to GOD that's one of the things I enjoy doing.

A lot of people look at me side eyed when I tell them that I am a morning person and the first thing that I want to do when I wake up is talk to HIM. In the mornings I thank him for waking me up for all the hope that he brings in my life, with doing that I'm sure that my day will be fulfilled with the opportunity to tell others how good he is to us all.

GOD is so amazing! You can pray to HIM anytime anywhere, that is what makes him so incredible. You don't have to make an appointment. You don't have to worry if HE is going to be late, you can call on HIM anytime of the day or night. One thing I know for sure HE will be there when you call.

I have no secrets with the LOVE I have for GOD. I share HIS goodness, his WORD, and most importantly the LOVE that HE shares with us all in every situation that a person may be faced with. I wouldn't be a very good coach if I didn't share the number one method that I know that will help in all areas of people's lives if they believe in HIM.

Prayer is powerful and it is not my intention to get up on a soap box and tell you what to pray for in your life. But I can tell you what prayer has done in my life and how it definitely works out better than any solution man has ever created. When you pray, you are able to leave all your worries with GOD which he will then leave you with peace. I am not saying that you can pray without any works in your life to improve your situation. But GOD wants to work with us and provide us with the strength, hope and encouragement to be in a place where we can receive his blessings.

There is no policy, regulation, set of laws, or rules in ways that we should pray to our CREATOR. Praying to GOD is just as easy as having a conversation with HIM to either thank HIM for something that has worked out in your favor or a time where you can place all of your burden and problems with HIM.

When we are actually engaged with GOD by reading HIS word and really believing in HIM that's when HE will put on our hearts our answers to our prayers and what direction we should move in.

We discussed earlier how we will be faced with temptation and other spiritual warfare tactics by the devil and prayer is what we should do when faced with the devils tactics so that he will flee from our tempted thoughts. A lot of times you will hear a person say that they are "prayed up" or "stay prayed up" which means that they have equipped themselves with GOD's word and spent time with him so that they are heavily armored and well protected from the devils tricks and games.

Praying is like being able to talk freely to GOD about whatever is on your mind; be it good or bad. It is the opportunity to express your feelings truthfully to HIM and the understanding that your thoughts are only with GOD and no one else.

GOD truly wants us to pray to HIM. There is nothing more pleasing to GOD when you want to have a conversation with him and pray to HIM for all of your needs. Never think that you are too busy for GOD or HE is too busy for you. There is never a time when you can't go to him in your time or need or just to say thank you.

Prayer definitely changes things for the better and I set off from the beginning of this book sharing with readers that we have been BORN TO CHANCE. Prayer is the one step of the process as we CHANGE our lives that cannot be left out of our daily lives for CHANGE to eventually occur in our lives.

This Is Not Forever

Everything in life has a start and end date on it. When problems arise they will seem as if they will be in your life forever, you will never be able to shake them if you don't find the strength to visualize the end of the process. While moving past the troubles with the Grace of GOD you will be able to overcome it all and see the blessings that are waiting on you.

When you turn your life over to GOD, and believe in HIS wonderful POWER and promises of HIS faithfulness to us, it will become easy to put your trust in HIS word and know beforehand that you will come out victorious at the end of your battles because you know HE forever has your back.

Sometimes we believe that we have made it through situations without any help whatsoever from GOD but that way of thinking couldn't be anything further from the truth. GOD has died on the cross for all of our sins and walking around thinking that you solved a problem all by yourself, that you were very concerned about is not being truthful to GOD. HE knows what you are doing and going through at all times, even before anything ever happens HE has your entire life already planned.

By studying his WORD you will learn that problems will not always last forever. When I read the WORD of GOD and instill HIS WORD in my everyday living my entire life becomes easier to navigate because I have learned who to believe in and realize who is in control of my life.

Today's world is backwards. People do not want to know GOD's goodness because they like the bad of the world too much. The world has taken over minds and everything that isn't good spiritually has been made to be the normal routine of our daily lives. Even though the world is made up of all type of sin, the sins have become accepted in our culture. No matter how normal they may seem they will turn into the spiritual realm and you will have to deal with GOD about them one way or another.

Being honest about what you are going through is also very important to do. Sometimes we like to mask and hide the things that are troubling or controlling our lives not for the better and when we do this, it only prolongs the pain and the time we have to endure as we are going through.

Being honest with GOD and yourself is most important if we have done things to get us in a particular situation. We must take it upon ourselves to do what we can do to right our wrongs. GOD comes to us with the truth and we have to be truthful to HIM while working our way to his kingdom so that we can be filled with HIS blessings that he has for our life here on earth.

GOD has promised us that he would never leave us nor forsake us, that's one of the reasons why we shouldn't be afraid to face whatever we are dealing with. Nobody likes to deal with bad news but if we know who is in control of the bad news then we aren't bound by it by becoming stressed out of our minds with panic.

For me and the belief I have in GOD, I know it is impossible for GOD to lie. So there is no reason for me to live in fear about problems that occur because HE is in the driver's seat taking care of everything for me. I very much believe in the power of GOD and I will continue to do that until the day I die.

Leaving the Past Behind

Our past can be a very dangerous thing in our lives. Things that have happened in our past can either be the best experiences ever or nightmares that we will never be able to shake. Past experiences help to shape our lives, there are many situations that we rely on the past to decide our future. The past can be so upsetting that it can stop us from moving forward and place our entire lives in a negative nose dive.

Leaving the past behind and moving on from being hurt is a very challenging feat that takes lots of PRAYER, a strong mind and will. When we are hurt the natural defensive mechanism is to turn around and hurt the one who has hurt us. Our instincts tell us to hurt them right back in order to get some type of peace and retribution from being wronged.

Leaving heartaches behind in the past takes forgiveness of the one who has hurt you. You might hear many people say that forgiveness is not necessarily just for you but it is also for the person that has hurt you and their well being and I can believe that as true.

Forgiveness is a must when dealing with past issues of hurt and pain in order to have PEACE in your life and the ability to move on without the issues affecting you in other areas of your life. If we continue to hold grudges against those who have wronged us, it automatically spills over into how we deal with other people who may come into our life, as well as those that are close to us. If we are constantly worrying about how we have been hurt from the past we will only clutter our minds and not be able to move ahead. We will also become upset about any little thing that reminds us of the past. We will be so irritable at the slightest things that we don't even realize that we are actually living our life with bitterness in our heart because of the past, that's why forgiveness is important.

There is a spiritual solution to any problem. Forgiveness is not something that just happens because the past is not easy to erase from your mind. There are way too many things in the world that can remind of us of our past and in order to really replace those thoughts and remove them you must use your spirituality and GOD to help you through.

There is no time limit on how long it will take to forgive someone. When you start out it will be difficult because anyone who attempts to come inside your world in the same capacity as you have been hurt you will automatically put up a barrier to that person just because of a bad past experience. I understand this but everyone is not out to hurt us and that's why we have to ask GOD to help us be wise in choosing those we let into our life. If there is a situation where you are attempting to continue in a personal or business relationship with someone who has hurt you, it will take time for all wounds to heal and both parties must be willing to understand that you have to go through putting the relationship back one day at a time.

Because forgiveness is such a huge undertaking for anyone to accomplish in their life, I have just briefly touched the basis of what it takes to forgive and some of the important topics and concerns that you will need in order to forgive. I will continue this discussion in my next book more in depth. I can say though that GOD and reading his WORD for forgiveness is most important. We have to remember that GOD has forgiven us for all of our sins and there is no way possible we can say that we believe in GOD and we can't forgive ourselves. AMEN.

Pointing Fingers

I will not sugar coat how many people blame someone else for their troubles and difficulties. I think as a teen parent of a divorced household I had just as much right to cast blame on a variety of people but I didn't and I have made the best of my circumstances and continue to make the best out of my choices in life.

I don't think people realize how easy it is to blame someone else for their problems and I also think there are some who think that they have the right to blame. I understand why they do it. They do it so that they won't look as bad as the situation appears if someone is at fault to garner some type of sympathy for not continuing on their path of life.

Looking in the mirror and honestly admitting how you have contributed to the problems at hand in your life is very important and a great start to realizing that whatever problem you find yourself in; you have played a part in it.

One of my main points about the blame game is that I think it is harder to place fault and give reasons why something is not going the way you really want it to– than taking some responsibility to what has happened in your life. Blaming is deep rooted and taking responsibility of your situation takes telling the truth which is part of looking in the mirror. It's like blaming those who are in front of you at a red light and the driver behind everyone is honking their horn and screaming and cursing everyone out because they are going to be late to their destination. There is no way you can blame everyone in front of you when you are to blame especially when you could have left the house earlier to make it on time.

Blaming others brings about many of the things that we should go to GOD to in order to rid ourselves from our own wrong doing. Blaming others for our problems brings stress and definitely fatigue to a point where a person becomes grouchy, unsettling and angry towards those in their life. Blame is very negative and is an emotion that does more harm than good. GOD does not give mercy to those who conceal their own transgressions. When you walk around in the world blaming everyone and everything on your situation and problems without admitting your own doing GOD is not pleased. GOD tells us to keep watch on your own self and HE does not want us to be hypocritical and not find our own fault in things that we are not happy about.

If you find yourself blaming others it would be a good idea to apologize for your part in the situation and ask GOD for directions to make what you are going through better.

GOD already knows that we aren't perfect and pointing fingers towards others is simply not the way to handle situations. In order to break this spiritual warfare we have to engrave in our minds over and over again that WE ARE RESPONSIBLE for our lives in every way and in every situation.

Change While Building A Support System

It is very important to have people in your circle who show love and support in all areas of your life. When you don't have people who are there for you that will stand with you and behind you, there's a chance that you will tend to let fear completely take over the situation you are going through. I have learned that some people are better fighters when they surround themselves with those that support them. They are more comfortable in the battle knowing their support will be with them at any given moment. They become much more motivated to handle their situations because they know they have the backup they need for their journey.

I keep the attitude of LOVE and support because that is just the way GOD made me to be. I don't have any other way of explaining it. I also want GOD to be proud of me so whatever I do or involved in I show love. I am not concerned if the world is proud of me or not. But when it is all said and done I want GOD to be proud of me of showing support and LOVE to those that HE has allowed me to be in contact with.

Sometimes it is difficult to actually show love and support for one another in a personal relationship or a business relationship. Many times people jump into relationships but aren't ready for a relationship or have not completely healed from a previous relationship. In a relationship loving yourself completely is necessary before you can bring anyone else into the equation. A lot of times in a relationship someone is looking for that certain validation that they think will make them feel whole as a person.

So many times relationships are rushed into without really understanding what a person is getting into. There are many people who jump into unions but know very little about the person they say they want to care for and be in their life. There has to be a thought process when you are getting into a relationship with someone just for the simple fact that you are taking some level of responsibility for that person and they are doing the same for you. There are many different personalities that we all have and they are not available for someone to read them directly off of our bodies like a billboard. When you first meet someone of course without a doubt they will be on their best behavior and say everything you want to hear. But truth be told you are only meeting that persons representative and later down the road you will eventually meet the actual person and more times than not they are not the same person you thought you knew.

The main purpose I am trying to get across here is that there are a lot of people who still think that someone else can fill in a part of their life where someone else has failed them. A fatherless female for example has a higher rate of falling for or to be in search of the strong male type that she has never experienced as a father. So it would be easy for this fatherless female to throw herself at men with these qualities and become hurt while making it a continuous cycle.

I would definitely ask of anyone looking for support and love to look at GOD for support. I know for a fact that HE will not only guide you in the right direction of goodness but will put the right people in your life who are full of encouragement, care and attention that have your best interest at heart.

Choices

Choices are different options at your disposal that you can choose from which basically have the right way to do something or the wrong way. Choices are very important when it comes to making decisions in your life and many choices that we make in our lives are made within seconds and are ones that we have to live with for the rest of our lives.

There are many who deal with strongholds in their life and prolong making very important decisions that will eventually affect them. When they finally decide to address the choices they need to make they have indulged in the stronghold for so long that it is not easy to execute a levelheaded choice because they have built a mess in their life and the stronghold has taken control.

We have discussed strongholds and spiritual warfare and I can't explain enough how all of these things are a continued cycle in life that all come together full circle that we all are forced to deal with. We make thousands of decisions and choices a day. Some are more important than others but we are still responsible in life to make a decision in seconds and then there are choices and decisions where we have the chance to sit down and think them out.

Out all of the decisions we have to make we– are either going to make the right one or the wrong one; there is no in-between. People are very scared of failure but for some reason always put themselves in a position to be failures with their choices.

I have really wondered whether or not if people truly understand the choices they make just don't only affect them. If they are in a relationship or married it affects everyone in the family and everyone they are responsible for. If it is a business decision it affects everyone who thinks they will have a job to come to day after day. That is the reason why it's so important to ask GOD to play a part in our decisions. Making choices is basically being responsible and looking into all the outcomes of the choice you make.

Too many times the selfish choices are being made and that is not GOD's purpose for our lives. If GOD has placed you head of your household and you are continually making selfish choices that only benefit you and the hunger in your own belly then you should leave the decision making to someone else because you're not able to make a wise choice. Making choices are for those who can lead, those that can lead themselves and others who look into the future and the consequences of the choice they have made.

I would be the first person to tell anyone who is being affected by someone who continually makes the wrong choices to make up their mind, no matter how much you love them, or care for them or want to be around them; to take a stance and let the person know they can no longer drag you with them and their unwise choices. I know it may be a difficult thing to do but staying with the person or an organization that constantly places you and your family at risk, is a stronghold that must be broken for you to be successful in life.

Obedience and Stepping Out on Faith

Throughout this book we have discussed so many different topics that I feel are very important in the terms of becoming an all round better person. Keep in mind I didn't say perfect because no one is perfect but GOD but it is what we all strive to be even though we know it is impossible to do so.

With that in mind, I would like to share how important OBEDIENCE is in order to try to obtain the GLORY that HE wants for us as we navigate through the world. For me, obedience to GOD means making sure you go through all the necessary steps to get a closer relationship with GOD and learn how to follow GOD while allowing yourself to understand that HE is leading you in every direction.

The act of OBEDIENCE is important and listening to your heart which GOD speaks through is important because there is a voice in each and every one of us and we hear it daily. But the fact of the matter is– do we listen to it? Being obedient to man instead of GOD is not the answer For example, if your license is suspended but you need extra money and a friend, asks you for a "favor" then offers you twenty dollars, to drive them up the street and you do it because it sounds good to have the extra money in your pocket. That means you have just obeyed man for the guidance of money, even though that voice you heard (GOD) was telling you not to, but instead, you do it anyway then end up getting pulled over by the police and locked up, because you didn't listen to your heart, which also disobeyed GOD.

If you haven't figured it out by now through the book that the devils intention is to have you moving in a circle, from strongholds to not being truthful to yourself, to choices and spiritual warfare. He will continue to have you rotating in the circle if you are not smart enough and strong enough to follow GOD so that you will be able to walk in the path GOD has for you.

Being obedient to GOD has to come with trust. You have to trust HIM and that leads to OBEDIENCE. A lot of people put their trust in man who always likes to throw money or something worldly in the equation to get you to be of the world. In my opinion way too many people are obedient to man instead of GOD and that is the main reason we have so many negative things on all types of levels attacking us because we have left the door wide open for the devil to come in our homes, businesses, relationships and families to take over and create confusion.

As we have discussed how important OBEDIENCE is it's also important that through this obedience and trust we step out on our faith to GOD. We need to be faithful to GOD in believing in HIM and also have FAITH that HE is leading the PATH we are on with him. FAITH is believing in the unseen. FAITH is believing and trusting that when we are in the midst of a storm we know that GOD will make us come out victorious. FAITH is knowing that whatever we ask of GOD if it is in HIS will HE will hear us and bless us.

FAITH is very motivating if you are a believer of GOD. Knowing that you have the greatest power known to mankind who is in your corner every second of your day who can do miraculous things at a blink of an eye is very motivating. It's like having the best basketball player on your team knowing that if the game get's close you are going to hand them the ball and watch them work for the win. That's what I want you to know about stepping out on faith. GOD can do anything HE desires and when you are obedient to Him and place all your FAITH in HIS hands there is no way you will lose.

Finding Self—Self love.....

What am I here for is a common question of those who are attempting to find themselves and the reasons they were placed here on earth. No one reading this book is a mistake. If you are reading this book there is a reason GOD gave you life and the talents you may or may not have uncovered to this point. Being on earth living in this world was not a mistake and if we listen to our hearts, souls, and spirits like we have discussed throughout the book you are well on your way of finding your true self.

The only way to finding yourself is to actually be your true self. Taking everything GOD has given you physically and mentally and owning it without any excuses. It is so important to be yourself so all your GOD given talents and abilities are able to shine through and manifest to show to others.

With all types of images and messages in the world circulating telling people what they should look like, act like, dress like, a person could become very lost in the world and confused to who they really are. That is why I will continue to say that to know GOD is to know yourself because with the love of GOD, his word and presence will only allow us to be ourselves. If we follow HIS direction for our life it will only let us be the way HE planned for our lives to be.

Developing into a well rounded individual does take time and doesn't happen overnight. It is a growing process where you will make mistakes learn from them and find out that you don't have to be put in bondage concerning your mistakes and you can make things better. I knew when I was a teen that having a child was a very big

91

responsibility and I have actually noticed the change I have made in my life not just about caring for my child but by learning more about myself. I have learned so much and feel as though this message that I am relaying to others who may be in the same tough situation as I was in gives some hope and motivation to know that you can come out of whatever type of situation you're in with the trust of GOD and working on finding yourself.

Evaluating what you're doing just like they do most employees on their jobs is the best way to getting the best out of situations and in to finding yourself. Learn what makes you happy. Learn what makes you feel good spiritually and physically. Find out if you are a morning person or a night person. I am a morning person and I realized that and appreciate the mornings because that is when I usually talk to GOD. The point is find what your likes and dislikes are and start day by day by removing the things that are not important in your life and not only partake in things that you do like but let others know what you like as well so they will get a better understanding of you too.

It is important to be firm when you are in the process of the journey of finding self and not be decisive and withholding who you are from others. Just like I will respect others I want the same respect back with the acknowledgment that everyone is not the same and those I associate with should appreciate that because I appreciate them for who they are. That's one of the reasons I feel people are afraid or have doubts about really finding out who they are because of the stronghold of fear and how they don't want others to judge and perceive them. If you don't know it yet there is no way you should let anyone else's perception of you stop you from doing anything or being what you want to be. Live your life the way GOD intended it to be lived and move by his voice. Understand that you are here on earth for a purpose and live in that purpose in LOVE.

Your Journey

We all have our own individual journey in life and our journeys are never ending while living on earth. Our journeys are filled with joy, challenges, sorrow and pain. We see many things occur through our own perception and the memories of these things we will always be able to hold close and remember.

There is a great misconception in life that we can live life without any challenges and worry free. But that is not the case, our journey is a complete challenge and it is up to us to understand this as we navigate through our time on earth and the way we navigate through it, is just as important as the journey itself.

For me challenges in life turn out to be a good thing. I think when someone is faced with a challenge it automatically takes them out of their comfort zone and it affects them big time because it takes someone out of their normal daily life. For example, if you purchase a new home after living in an apartment for several years, there is going to be an adjustment period. There is a possibility that you will not sleep as well as you did in your old home and you have to challenge yourself to become comfortable in your new surroundings.

You will come to find out through your journey of life that your journey will build your character. Life's experiences can do a 360 and you won't even believe how far you have grown once you look back at it. Your journey also builds your faith in GOD. You will realize and see how things may not have been so good for you at a particular point. But when you look back at it and wonder how you were able to get through storms you were faced with, that is truly when you realize the goodness of GOD.

The journey that I have traveled in my life has definitely built my faith. As I look back at how I have come out of strongholds and spiritual warfare and the days I felt like giving up then seeing GOD go to work in my life it has strengthen my FAITH. Through my own journey I know how important it is to stay positive and believe that things will turn out for the better. It is just so much easier to be negative when we are moving forward and that is where the blame game we talked about occurs. If we continue to pick out everything negative during our journey then we will never be able to accomplish the journey. But having a strong mental mindset and the support system that I discussed will help on your journey.

Our dreams are so much very apart of our journey. We have to have dreams in order to set off on a journey. My dream to be a motivational speaker and help people to understand self love and to be able to have a relationship with GOD lets me know that we have the power to make it happen. When you have no control of your journey it's just like letting the devil take you on a ride until he is finished being bothered with you. I see so many people who are unhappy in their life's journey because they have let life control them. When life controls you then you are following someone else's journey and not totally being yourself.

I have enjoyed my journey because I have learned so much about myself and I thank GOD for it. I look back and say that if I have not gone through my past I would more than likely to this day still be making the bad choices and decisions. If I didn't grasp onto the negative things and intentionally turn them into positives, I don't know where my life would be.

Living life like an adventure is what I try to do. I place my mindset on a cruise ship and enjoy each wave and ripple that comes along with the ride of life. I know if I do this I will end up loving my entire journey of life. I do this because I don't want to become old and have to look back on my life and see all of the things I thought about doing but never took the time or the chance to do it. For me this is about building great memories of my life and looking back one day to review my journey and receive more perspective into it. As I continue to live my life, I hope everyone joins me as I smile and praise GOD. Join me as I continue to show and give LOVE to all those that may cross my path. I want those who really don't understand why Tiffany always has a smile on her face and is in an upbeat positive mood to know that it is real and I have a reason for it. I am enjoying my journey and it is only because I have accepted GOD in my life and I have been BORN TO CHANGE.

About the Author

Tiffany Robinson is a Hampton, Virginia native currently residing in Atlanta, Georgia with her loving husband and two amazing daughters.

Tiffany credits being raised in a two-parent home where there was an abundance of love and attention as her foundation. Her childhood was picture perfect...until the day her parents announced they were getting a divorce.

Unexpectedly, her perfect world was turned upside down and filled with turmoil and angst. Tiffany suffered from depression, faced unimaginable challenges, and unexpected changes throughout her teenage years. She often asked herself, "Why me?"

Looking back, Tiffany understands all of the heartache and pain she endured was a necessary journey for her to learn compassion, humility, and to strengthen her relationship with God.

Today, Tiffany Robinson fully devotes herself to helping others who are in need of guidance, resolve, enlightenment, and a sense of purpose. It's her passion to help her clients find their breakthrough to a better life and to see their dreams become a reality. Not only does it give her a sense of purpose, Tiffany finds the experience of helping others incredibly rewarding.

If you would like to schedule a session for life coaching or a speaking, please go visit her website @ TiffanyTooReal.com Please feel free to follow her on twitter and Instagram @TiffanyTooReal. Please like her Facebook page@TiffanyTooReal